DAD JOKE LOADING...

DAD JOKE LOADING

This edition copyright © Octopus Publishing Group Limited, 2025
First published as *The Bumper Book of Jokes* in 2017

All rights reserved.

No part of this book may be reproduced by any means, nor transmitted, nor translated into a machine language, without the written permission of the publishers.

Condition of Sale
This book is sold subject to the condition that it shall not, by way of trade or otherwise, be lent, resold, hired out or otherwise circulated in any form of binding or cover other than that in which it is published and without a similar condition including this condition being imposed on the subsequent purchaser.

An Hachette UK Company
www.hachette.co.uk

Summersdale Publishers
Part of Octopus Publishing Group Limited
Carmelite House
50 Victoria Embankment
LONDON
EC4Y 0DZ
UK

www.summersdale.com

This FSC® label means that materials and other controlled sources used for the product have been responsibly sourced

The authorized representative in the EEA is Hachette Ireland, 8 Castlecourt Centre, Dublin 15, D15 XTP3, Ireland (email: info@hbgi.ie)

Printed and bound in Poland

ISBN: 978-1-83799-697-1
eISBN: 978-1-83799-698-8

Substantial discounts on bulk quantities of Summersdale books are available to corporations, professional associations and other organizations. For details contact general enquiries: telephone: +44 (0) 1243 771107 or email: enquiries@summersdale.com.

DAD JOKE LOADING...

The Ultimate Collection for "Funny" Fathers

summersdale

How do you make anti-freeze?

Steal her pyjamas.

MY GRANDFATHER HAS THE HEART OF A LION AND A LIFETIME BAN FROM THE LOCAL ZOO.

If you have trouble getting your children's attention, just sit down and look comfortable.

According to children, the perfect amount of time to stay at the park is five more minutes.

Why did the cat run from the tree?

Because it was afraid of the bark.

Why was the birthday cake as hard as a rock?

Because it was a marble cake.

When should you buy a bird?

When it's going cheep.

Child: The referee sent me off.

Mum: What for?

Child: The rest of the game.

New gardeners learn
by trowel and error.

If I could only grow green
stuff in my garden like
I can in my fridge.

What goes up and never comes down?

Your age!

TWO TELEVISION AERIALS MET ON A ROOFTOP, FELL IN LOVE AND GOT MARRIED. THE CEREMONY WAS AWFUL, BUT THE RECEPTION WAS EXCELLENT.

Whenever I go
near my bank, I get
withdrawal symptoms.

My email password has been
hacked. That's the third time
I've had to rename the cat.

Why do seagulls fly over the sea?

Because if they flew over the bay, they would be bagels.

Why couldn't Dracula's wife get to sleep?

Because of his coffin.

How do you tell when a mid-engined Ferrari is warmed up?

It's on fire.

Patient: Doctor, I get heartburn every time I eat birthday cake.

Doctor: Next time, make sure you take off the candles.

Don't trust atoms...
they make up everything.

A computer lets you make more mistakes faster than any invention in human history — with the possible exceptions of handguns and tequila.

Why did the cow go in the spaceship?

It wanted to see the moooooooon.

AN ORANGE AND AN APPLE SIGNED UP FOR A TENNIS TOURNAMENT. NO ONE WAS SURPRISED TO FIND OUT THEY WERE BOTH SEEDED.

I was going to look for my missing watch, but I could never find the time.

The bride weeps, the bridesmaids cry — even the wedding cake is in tiers.

What did the fisherman say to the card magician?

Take a cod, any cod.

Where do birds invest their money?

In the stork market.

What do you call a fake noodle?

An impasta.

Teacher: How many seconds are there in a year?

Pupil: Twelve! January the 2nd, February the 2nd...

Sleeping comes so naturally to me, I could do it with my eyes closed.

I do ten sit-ups every morning. It might not sound like much, but there are only so many times you can hit the snooze button.

What is a dog's favourite city?

New Yorkie.

I SAW AN ADVERT FOR BURIAL PLOTS AND THOUGHT TO MYSELF: THIS IS THE LAST THING I NEED.

When a psychic showed me the person I'll marry, it was love at second sight.

They say a lot of people die because of alcohol, but they don't realize how many people are also born because of it.

Why did the hamster die?

He fell asleep at the wheel.

What is a vampire's favourite holiday?

Fangsgiving.

Old chemistry teachers never die.

They just fail to react.

Big Brother: That planet over there is Mars.

Little Brother: Then that other one must be Pa's.

The clock was still hungry, so it went back four seconds.

If you plant pasta and water it with alcohol, a university student will grow.

What do you call Santa Claus when he stops moving?

Santa Pause.

I LIVE IN CONSTANT FEAR THAT MY CHILD WILL BECOME A FAMOUS ARTIST AND I WILL HAVE THROWN OUT ABOUT A MILLION POUNDS' WORTH OF THEIR WORK.

Nature abhors a vacuum, but not as much as a cat does.

According to my boss, "sick of being here" is not a valid reason to go home sick.

Don't worry about avoiding temptation.

As you grow older, it will avoid you.

Why did the computer get cold?

Because it forgot to close Windows.

Did you hear about the thief who stole a calendar?

He got 12 months.

Professor: What inspired you to write this essay?

Student: The deadline.

Parenting is mostly just informing kids how many more minutes they have of something.

My neighbour asked if he could use my lawnmower and I told him, of course he could, so long as he didn't take it out of my garden.

Did you hear about the new restaurant on the moon?

Great food but no atmosphere.

A NEUTRON WALKED INTO A BAR AND ASKED, "HOW MUCH IS A PINT?" THE BARTENDER SMILED AND REPLIED, "FOR YOU, NO CHARGE."

A toast to bread!
For without bread, there
could be no toast.

I'll tell you what I love
doing more than anything
— trying to pack myself
in a small suitcase. I can
hardly contain myself.

Why did the banana go to the doctor?

Because it wasn't peeling well.

Why do the French like to eat snails?

Because they don't like fast food.

Why do demons and ghouls hang out together?

Because demons are a ghoul's best friend!

Detective: Why did you dump those vegetables on my desk?

Criminal: You said it was time to spill the beans!

When I was a kid I had two friends, and they were imaginary and they would only play with each other.

University is where you question how on Earth you were able to wake up at 7 a.m. every day in secondary school.

What is a cat's way of keeping order?

Claw enforcement.

ARTIFICIAL INTELLIGENCE IS AN INCREDIBLE THING. I TOLD MY COMPUTER THAT TODAY IS MY BIRTHDAY. IT TOLD ME THAT I NEEDED AN UPGRADE.

Life and beer are very similar: chill for best results.

The worst part about being a birthday cake is when you're set on fire and then eaten by the hero that saved you.

Why did the rubber chicken cross the road?

She wanted to stretch her legs.

What kind of TV do you find inside a haunted house?

A wide-scream TV.

Why can male elephants swim whenever they want?

They always have trunks with them.

Man: I'd like to open a joint account please.

Cashier: OK, with whom?

Man: Whoever has the most money.

I'll never forget my grandfather's last words: "Stop shaking the ladder, you idiot!"

Two fish are in a tank. One says to the other: "Can you drive this thing?"

Which fish can perform operations?

A sturgeon.

A SNAIL WAS MUGGED IN AN ALLEY BY TWO SLUGS. LATER A DETECTIVE ASKED HIM FOR A DESCRIPTION OF THE ASSAILANTS. "I'M NOT SURE," SAID THE SNAIL, "IT ALL HAPPENED SO FAST."

I say no to alcohol —
it just doesn't listen.

Two lions were strolling
down a street. One turned
to the other and said,
"Not many people around
today, are there?"

Why don't eggs tell jokes?

They'd crack each other up.

What do you call a cashew in a spacesuit?

An astronut.

Why did the cookie cry?

Because his mother had been a wafer so long.

Guest: Does the water always come through the roof like that?

Hotel manager: No, sir. Only when it rains.

To become a pilot requires a good altitude.

There are three signs of old age. The first is your loss of memory. I forget the other two.

What do you call a flying primate?

A hot-air baboon.

UNIVERSITY IS A LOT LIKE PRESCHOOL. YOU SLEEP A LOT, MISS YOUR MUM AND HAVE NO CLUE WHAT'S GOING ON.

Age is only important if you're cheese or wine.

Two wrongs don't make a right — take me and your mother as an example.

What are twins' favourite fruit?

Pears.

What kind of chocolate do they sell at the airport?

Plane chocolate.

Why did the vegan go deep-sea fishing?

Just for the halibut.

Father: Aren't you first in anything at school?

Child: Yes, Dad. I'm first out when the bell rings.

The manicurist just gave birth to a son. She called him Hans.

You know you're getting old when your back goes out more than you do.

What do angry rodents send each other for Christmas?

Cross mouse cards.

GETTING DRUNK AT THE PUB IS NOT THE ANSWER, UNLESS YOU'RE ASKING WHAT I'M DOING THIS WEEKEND.

Helicopter rescue pilots have the most successful pick-up lines.

When you're wearing a watch on a plane, time flies.

Why did the picture go to prison?

Because it was framed.

Why did the fungi leave the party?

There wasn't mushroom.

Why couldn't the student divide by two?

They didn't know the half of it.

Jane: I'd love to be a TV actress.

Harry: Break a leg!

Jane: What? Why?

Harry: Then you'd be in a cast for weeks.

Ninety per cent of a relationship is figuring out where to eat.

There was an awful fight at the seafood restaurant – four fish got battered!

Where do sharks go on holiday?

Finland.

DID YOU HEAR ABOUT THE DOG WHO ATE NOTHING BUT GARLIC? HIS BARK WAS MUCH WORSE THAN HIS BITE.

Time flies like an arrow,
but fruit flies like a banana.

Statistics show that teen
pregnancies drop off
significantly after age 25.

Why are fish never good tennis players?

They don't like getting close to the net.

What do you get when you cross a computer with a lifeguard?

A screensaver.

What does bread do on its summer holidays?

It just loafs around.

Patient: Doctor, doctor, I can't get to sleep.

Doctor: Sit on the edge of the bed and you'll soon drop off.

I love pressing F5 on my keyboard – it's so refreshing.

Bankers never give up; they just lose interest.

Why should you never break up with a goalie?

They're a keeper.

DID YOU HEAR OXYGEN WENT ON A DATE WITH POTASSIUM? IT WENT OK.

The older I get, the earlier it gets late.

If time is money, are ATMs time machines?

What did one plate say to the other?

Lunch is on me!

Why don't ducks tell jokes when they fly?

Because they would quack up.

Why did the elephant cross the road?

To prove he wasn't chicken.

Teacher: What did Henry VIII do when he came to the throne?

Pupil: He sat on it.

I like birthdays, but too many can kill you.

My neighbours have been listening to music all night – I love my stereo.

What's green and sings?

Elvis Parsley.

I WENT TO THE BANK THE OTHER DAY AND ASKED THE CASHIER TO CHECK MY BALANCE, SO THEY PUSHED ME AND ASKED HOW I FELT.

The cat wore a dress
because it was feline fine.

The game of golf is
90 per cent mental and
10 per cent mental.

What is the most important thing a witch learns in school?

Spelling.

What did the horse say to the foal?

It's pasture bedtime.

Why don't aliens eat clowns?

Because they taste funny!

Caller: Finally! I got through! I've been trying to call the zoo for hours!

Zookeeper: Yes, all our lions were busy.

The conceited watch was a bit too clocky.

Shoplifters are the strongest kind of thief.

What do Christmas trees do when winter is over?

They pine a lot.

AT THE LOCAL PETTING ZOO, I SAW A SHEEP SCRATCHING ITSELF. TURNS OUT IT HAD FLEECE.

Lumberjacks love logging into computers.

The owl lost its voice but didn't give a hoot, apparently.

Which animal always comes top in exams?

The cheetah.

How many magicians does it take to change a light bulb?

It depends on what you want it changed into...

What do stylish frogs wear?

Jumpsuits!

Diner: Are you sure this place is hygienic?

Manager: Yes, sir. You could eat off the floor.

Diner: That's the problem. It looks as if somebody has!

When a chemist dies,
you have to barium.

I just got skylights put in my place and the neighbours upstairs are furious.

What did the clothing manufacturer call her daughter?

Polly-Esther.

SOME AQUATIC MAMMALS AT THE ZOO ESCAPED. IT WAS OTTER CHAOS.

Be nice to your kids; they'll choose your nursing home.

Organic chemistry is difficult — those who study it have alkynes of trouble.

What do baby dogs eat at the cinema?

Pupcorn.

What's the best thing to put into a pie?

Your teeth!

What kind of doctor fixes broken websites?

A URLologist.

Teacher: Which two days of the week start with the letter "t"?

Pupil: Today and tomorrow.

I'd tell you the joke about the staccato, but it's too short.

I've seen it all, done it all and can't remember most of it.

Why do ducks fly south?

Because it's too far to walk.

FORGET ABOUT THE PAST, YOU CAN'T CHANGE IT. FORGET ABOUT THE FUTURE, YOU CAN'T PREDICT IT. FORGET ABOUT THE PRESENT, I DIDN'T GET YOU ONE.

The goose was sent off
the pitch for fowl play.

If you sit on your watch
you'll always be on time.

What kind of cat will keep your grass short?

A lawn meower.

Did you hear about the wall that went out on the town for its birthday?

It got plastered.

What do computers like to eat?

Chips.

Customer: I bought this computer yesterday and I found a twig in the disk drive!

Employee: I'm sorry, sir, you'll have to speak to the branch manager.

An optimist is a student who opens their wallet and expects to find money.

Marriage can be like a hot bath; the longer you stay in, the colder it gets.

What do you get when you cross a snake and a plane?

A Boeing constrictor.

SOMEONE KEEPS DUMPING SOIL ALL OVER MY ALLOTMENT, AND I DON'T KNOW WHO'S DOING IT. THE PLOT THICKENS.

I dressed up as a frog and robbed a bank. They say I Kermit-ted a crime.

The new bamboo trees at the zoo are causing panda-monium.

Why did the teacher wear sunglasses to work?

Because his class was so bright.

How many tennis players does it take to change a light bulb?

What do you mean it was out? It was in!

What kind of dog can tell the time?

A watchdog.

Father: Why is there a strange baby in the crib?

Child: You told me to change the baby.

Frogs like wearing shoes, especially open-toad sandals.

The skeleton wasn't very nice – he told the vampire he sucked.

What did one quantum physicist say when he started to fight another quantum physicist?

Let me atom!

FIVE HUNDRED HARES HAVE ESCAPED FROM THE ZOO, SO THE POLICE ARE BUSY COMBING THE AREA.

Birds of prey spend a lot of time on their knees.

The man took a measuring tape to bed with him to measure how long he slept.

Why did the rooster cross the road?

To cock-a-doodle-doo something.

How do chickens get strong?

Egg-cercise.

Why didn't the elephant buy a suitcase for its holiday?

Because it already had a trunk.

Teacher: Do you have trouble making decisions?

Pupil: Well... yes and no.

The tomato turned red because it saw the salad dressing.

There are two kinds of lawyers: those who know the law and those who know the judge.

Why do dogs run
in circles?

Because it's hard to
run in squares.

MY GRANDMOTHER STARTED WALKING FIVE MILES A DAY WHEN SHE WAS 60 YEARS OLD. NOW SHE'S 97 AND WE DON'T KNOW WHERE SHE IS.

Apparently, ancient Egyptian mummies loved listening to wrap music.

One boat asked another boat if they were interested in row-mance.

How do snowmen get to work?

By icicle.

What did the tennis ball say when it got hit?

Who's making all the racquet?

What's grey, squeaky and hangs around in caves?

Stalagmice.

Father: Why was your exam score so low last week?

Child: Absence.

Father: What, you missed the exam?

Child: No, but the girl who sits next to me did.

The moon knows it's had enough to eat when it's full.

I've heard that zombies prefer to go swimming in the Dead Sea.

What time is it when you sit on a pin?

Springtime.

"AGEING GRACEFULLY" IS LIKE THE NICE WAY OF SAYING YOU'RE SLOWLY LOOKING WORSE.

THE DAD ANNUAL

The ultimate compendium of hilarious games, bad jokes, mind-boggling trivia and much, much more!

Michael Spicer

THE DAD ANNUAL
Michael Spicer

Hardback
ISBN: 978-1-78783-298-5

Bursting with puzzles, quizzes, trivia and games, this dad-tastic annual packs in hours of fun for fathers everywhere!

Whether you're keen to know where you rank on the leader board of all-time cool dads, want to try your hand at some perplexing puzzles or you just want to add some new dad-dancing moves to your already extensive repertoire, this annual does it all!

Have you enjoyed this book? If so, find us on Facebook at **Summersdale Publishers**, on Twitter/X at **@Summersdale** and on Instagram, TikTok and Bluesky at **@summersdalebooks** and get in touch. We'd love to hear from you!

www.summersdale.com

Image credits

pp.6, 14, 22, 30, 38, 46, 54, 62, 70, 78, 86, 94, 102, 110, 118, 126, 134, 142, 150 – moustache icon © TotemArt/Shutterstock.com

pp.8, 16, 24, 32, 40, 48, 56, 64, 72, 80, 88, 96, 104, 112, 120, 128, 136, 144, 152 – tie icon © lalan/Shutterstock.com

pp.4, 12, 20, 28, 36, 44, 52, 60, 68, 76, 84, 92, 100, 108, 116, 124, 132, 140, 148, 156 – glasses icon © Rauf Aliyev/Shutterstock.com

pp.11, 19, 27, 35, 43, 51, 59, 67, 75, 83, 91, 99, 107, 115, 123, 131, 139, 147, 155 – bow tie icon © Francois Poirier/Shutterstock.com

pp.7, 15, 23, 31, 39, 47, 55, 63, 71, 79, 87, 95, 103, 111, 119, 127, 135, 143, 151 – hat icon © Emeraldora/Shutterstock.com

pp.9, 17, 25, 33, 41, 49, 57, 65, 73, 81, 89, 97, 105, 113, 121, 129, 137, 145, 153 – tools icon © TotemArt/Shutterstock.com

pp.10, 18, 26, 34, 42, 50, 58, 66, 74, 82, 90, 98, 106, 114, 122, 130, 138, 146, 154 – loading bar icon © rajjdesign/Shutterstock.com